THE
Junior Chef
COOKBOOK

DEVELOPED BY
WILLIAMS
SONOMA
TEST KITCHEN

photographs Maren Caruso

weldon**owen**

Contents

Introducing Junior Chef Cooking

Spending time in the kitchen and creating delicious food to share is a great way to learn cooking skills, especially when you are young. With the guidance of family and friends, learning to cook at an early age will shape the way you cook and eat for years to come. And besides, preparing a tasty meal from a handful of ingredients and then sitting down to enjoy the food together is rewarding and fun. It will also give you a big sense of accomplishment.

This collection of easy-to-prepare recipes, a companion book to Williams-Sonoma's popular Junior Chef cooking class series, will inspire you to explore and create in the kitchen. Discover how easy it is to prepare scrumptious, satisfying dishes with fresh ingredients. Classic recipes, like omelets, pancakes, pizza, Caesar salad, and more, will teach you invaluable cooking techniques that you can use throughout your life. Favorite dishes are given a fun twist, like Cheddar & Gruyère Mac 'n' Cheese with bacon and a crispy-crunchy panko crust (page 23), Garlic & Herb Pull-Apart Bread (page 42), Egg-in-a-Hole Sandwiches with Maple-Glazed Bacon (page 20), and Chocolate Pretzel–Dipped Cookies (page 56).

You'll also find plenty of ideas for tempting weekday family breakfasts and dinners, brown bag lunches, and snacks, including fried chicken, guacamole, baked sweet potato fries, and brownies with peanut butter swirl. From morning to night, *The Junior Chef Cookbook* will give you not only a wealth of recipes but also tips on how to read a recipe, stay organized in the kitchen, and keep safe while you cook.

Continually clean your cutting board, especially after cutting spicy or messy ingredients.

Measure the amount of food you'll need for the recipe, and keep it in tidy, separate piles.

A variety of different sized bowls keeps prepped food neatly organized.

Prepare to Cook

Now that you have a cookbook filled with inspiring recipes that you can't wait to make and eat, you are probably ready to get started! But before you dive in and begin cooking, here are some tips for keeping things fun—and well organized—in the kitchen:

1. Carefully read the entire recipe so you know what to expect.

2. Make sure you have enough time to make the recipe so you don't have to rush through any of it.

3. Clear off a workspace in the kitchen that's big enough to prepare the dish and work comfortably.

4. Gather your cooking equipment, tools, and ingredients. This is called *mise en place*, which is French for "everything in its place."

5. Before you start to cook, measure out all of the ingredients. This will make preparation easier and will also ensure that you have everything you need to make the dish.

6. Rinse and dry any fruits and vegetables prior to chopping or slicing them as directed in the recipe.

7. Keep your workspace clean, neat, and tidy as you cook. Move bowls, pans, and cooking tools to the sink as you finish with them.

Playing It Safe

Cooking is an activity that everyone can enjoy!
But it's important to learn about kitchen safety in order
to become a confident, independent cook. Here are
some tips for staying safe:

- **Always ask an adult for help** when you have questions
  or need assistance, especially when using the stove top,
  oven, and kitchen appliances, and whenever you need
  to use a knife or other sharp tools.

- **Be extra careful** with sharp knives and tools.

- **Wash your hands** with warm soapy water before
  cooking or handling ingredients and after touching
  raw meat or fish.

- **Roll up your sleeves** and wear an apron or chef's jacket
  to keep your clothes clean.

- **Tie back your hair** if it's long to keep it out of the way.

- **Always stay in the kitchen** if you have something on
  the stove top or in the oven. It's a good idea to set a
  timer so you don't forget to check if your dish is ready.

- **Use thick, dry oven mitts** when handling anything
  that is hot in order to protect your hands from burns.
  (Wet mitts or towels will burn!)

- **Let hot pans cool** before moving them to the sink
  or washing them.

Blueberry-Almond Muffins

Rise and shine to blueberry muffins! A hint of almond makes these extra special. The brown sugar streusel is optional—the muffins are delicious either way.

1 Preheat the oven to 375°F. Grease 12 standard muffin cups or line with paper liners.

2 If making the streusel, in a bowl, stir together the flour, almonds, brown sugar, and salt. Using clean fingers, mix in the butter until the streusel is moist and crumbly. Set aside.

3 To make the muffins, in a bowl, whisk together the flour, baking powder, and salt. Set aside.

4 In the bowl of a stand mixer fitted with the paddle attachment, beat together the butter and brown sugar on medium speed until light and fluffy. Add the eggs 1 at a time and beat until fully incorporated. Slowly add the yogurt in 2 additions and then both extracts, beating until combined.

5 Reduce the speed to low and add the flour mixture in 2 additions and beat until combined. Remove the bowl from the mixer and gently fold in the blueberries. Divide the batter between the prepared muffin cups and sprinkle with the streusel, if using.

6 Bake until the muffins are lightly golden and set, about 25 minutes. Let the muffins cool in the pan on a wire rack for 10–15 minutes, then turn them out onto the rack and let cool completely.

For the streusel (optional)

¼ cup all-purpose flour

¼ cup sliced almonds

2 tablespoons firmly packed light brown sugar

Pinch of kosher salt

3 tablespoons cold unsalted butter

For the muffins

2 cups all-purpose flour

2 teaspoons baking powder

½ teaspoon kosher salt

½ cup unsalted butter, at room temperature

1 cup firmly packed light brown sugar

2 large eggs

½ cup full-fat plain yogurt

1 teaspoon vanilla extract

½ teaspoon almond extract

1½ cups fresh or frozen blueberries tossed with 1 tablespoon all-purpose flour

The compote can also be made with other fruits or berries: Try it with blueberries or pitted cherries.

Buttermilk Pancakes with Berry Compote

Whip up a batch of these pancakes on the weekend and we guarantee your family will ask for a repeat performance! Take care not to overmix the batter—you'll end up with tough pancakes.

1 To make the compote, in a saucepan, stir together the raspberries, blackberries, strawberries, sugar, and lemon juice. Place over medium heat and bring to a simmer. Cook, stirring occasionally, until most of the berries have broken down and the mixture is thickened, about 15 minutes; reduce the heat if the compote sticks to the pan. Let the compote cool to room temperature. Use right away or store in an airtight container in the refrigerator for up to 1 week.

2 To make the pancakes, preheat the oven to 200°F. In a large bowl, whisk the eggs until frothy. Add the flour, sugar, baking powder, baking soda, salt, buttermilk, butter, and vanilla. Stir just until the batter is smooth and no lumps remain; do not overmix.

3 Carefully heat a griddle or a nonstick frying pan over medium-high heat until a few drops of water flicked onto the surface skitter across it. Lightly grease the griddle with a little of the oil.

4 Using a batter dispenser set on the large setting or a medium ladle, dispense the batter onto the griddle. Cook until bubbles form on top and the batter is set, 1–2 minutes. Using a spatula, flip the pancakes and cook until golden brown on the other side, 2–3 minutes longer. Transfer to a baking sheet and keep warm in the oven. Repeat to cook the remaining pancakes.

5 Serve the pancakes with maple syrup and the compote.

For the berry compote

1 pint fresh raspberries

1 pint fresh blackberries

1 pint fresh strawberries, hulled

2 tablespoons sugar

2 teaspoons fresh lemon juice

For the pancakes

2 large eggs

2 cups all-purpose flour, sifted

3 tablespoons sugar

2 teaspoons baking powder

1 teaspoon baking soda

1 teaspoon kosher salt

2¼ cups buttermilk

4 tablespoons unsalted butter, melted

½ teaspoon vanilla extract

1–2 tablespoons vegetable oil

Maple syrup, for serving

Traditional French Omelet

This omelet calls for *fines herbes*, a combination of parsley, chives, tarragon, and chervil traditionally used in French cooking, but other fresh herbs will also work well. Try different kinds of cheese if you like.

1 In a small bowl, stir together the parsley, chives, tarragon, and chervil.

2 Place an omelet pan or medium nonstick frying pan over medium heat. In a small bowl, whisk together 2 of the eggs, a pinch of salt, and a few grindings of pepper. Stir in 1 tablespoon of the herb mixture.

3 Brush ½ tablespoon of the melted butter on the bottom of the pan and pour in the egg mixture. Using a rubber spatula, push the eggs from the edges of the pan toward the center and gently tilt the pan to evenly redistribute the uncooked eggs. Repeat until the eggs are just set and cover the bottom of the pan, 1–2 minutes. Sprinkle 1 tablespoon of the cheese over the top and cook just until the cheese is melted and the eggs are fully cooked, about 1 minute longer. Use the spatula to fold the omelet in half and slide onto a plate.

4 Repeat to cook 3 more omelets. Garnish the omelets with more herbs and cheese. Serve warm.

1 tablespoon finely chopped fresh flat-leaf parsley, plus more for garnish

1 tablespoon finely chopped fresh chives, plus more for garnish

1 tablespoon finely chopped fresh tarragon, plus more for garnish

1 tablespoon finely chopped fresh chervil, plus more for garnish

8 large eggs

Kosher salt and freshly ground pepper

2 tablespoons unsalted butter, melted

4 tablespoons grated Cheddar cheese, plus more for garnish

Homemade Cheesy Crackers

Salty, crunchy, cheesy, and totally addictive! You just might want to make a double batch of these crisp treats. Try different cheese combinations or mix in finely chopped herbs like thyme or rosemary.

1 In a food processor, combine the flour, salt, and Parmesan and pulse until the mixture resembles coarse meal. Add the Cheddar and butter and pulse until the mixture is fine and crumbly. With the processor running, slowly add the ice water 1 tablespoon at a time until the dough comes together when pressed with your hand.

2 Turn the dough out onto a work surface, divide it in half, and shape each into a flat square. Wrap each square tightly with plastic wrap and refrigerate for about 1 hour or up to overnight.

3 Preheat the oven to 375°F. Cut 2 sheets of parchment paper the size of a baking sheet and dust with flour. Working directly on the parchment, roll out each dough square ⅛ inch thick. Sprinkle with sea salt flakes and cut into individual 1-inch squares. A straight or fluted pizza cutter and a ruler are helpful for this step.

4 Transfer the parchment with the crackers to 2 baking sheets and place in the freezer for 10 minutes. Remove from the freezer and bake until the crackers are puffed and golden brown, 12–15 minutes, carefully rotating the baking sheets 180 degrees halfway through baking. Let cool completely in the pan. The crackers can be stored in a sealed container for up to 3 days.

1 cup all-purpose flour, plus more for dusting

½ teaspoon kosher salt

1½ oz Parmesan cheese, grated

½ lb sharp Cheddar cheese, cut into cubes

4 tablespoons cold unsalted butter, cut into 1-inch pieces

2–3 tablespoons ice water, plus more as needed

Sea salt flakes

Egg-in-a-Hole Sandwiches with Maple-Glazed Bacon

By cooking the egg within the toast, this classic breakfast sandwich gets an updated twist. A glaze of sweet maple syrup makes the bacon irresistible. Spice lovers will enjoy a dash of hot sauce on their sandwich.

1 Place 1 rack in the upper third and 1 rack in the lower third of the oven and preheat to 375°F. Line a baking sheet with parchment paper.

2 Place the bacon in a single layer on the parchment-lined sheet. Bake on the bottom oven rack for 15 minutes. Carefully remove the baking sheet from the oven and brush the bacon on both sides with the maple syrup, using tongs to flip them. Continue baking until the bacon is crispy, about 5 minutes longer.

3 Meanwhile, generously grease another baking sheet with butter. Spread butter on both sides of the bread slices. Using a 2½-inch round cookie cutter or a glass, cut a hole out of the center of 4 of the bread slices (toast the centers for a snack or save for making bread crumbs). Place all of the bread slices on the prepared baking sheet and toast on the top oven rack until lightly browned, 6 minutes.

4 Carefully remove the baking sheet from the oven, then flip the bread slices over and crack 1 egg into each hole. Sprinkle the eggs with salt and pepper and bake for 5 minutes. Carefully remove the baking sheet from the oven, place the cheese on the 4 slices without the eggs, and bake until the cheese is melted, 3–4 minutes longer.

5 To assemble each sandwich, cut 2 bacon slices in half crosswise and place on a cheesy bread slice, then cover with an egg-in-the-hole, egg facing up. Serve warm.

8 thick slices bacon

¼ cup maple syrup

3 tablespoons unsalted butter, at room temperature, plus more for greasing

8 slices sourdough bread

4 large eggs

Kosher salt and freshly ground pepper

1 cup grated Cheddar cheese

Cheddar & Gruyère Mac 'n' Cheese

This mac 'n' cheese is extra rich and cheesy because the recipe uses béchamel sauce, made by whisking together butter and flour and then incorporating milk, half-and-half, and cheese.

1 Preheat the oven to 425°F. Bring a large saucepan of salted water to a boil over high heat. Carefully add the pasta and cook, stirring occasionally, until not quite al dente (tender but firm to the bite), about 2 minutes less than the package instructions. Drain and transfer to a large bowl.

2 In the same saucepan over medium-high heat, melt the butter. Add the flour and cook, stirring well, until it is thoroughly incorporated, 1–3 minutes. Whisk in the milk, half-and-half, nutmeg, and a generous pinch of salt and bring to a boil. Simmer, whisking frequently to smooth out any lumps, for 4–5 minutes, until slightly thickened. Remove from the heat. Add a pinch of pepper and two-thirds each of the Gruyère and Cheddar. Stir until smooth.

3 Pour the cheese sauce over the pasta and stir well. Divide the pasta mixture between six 4-oz ramekins. Top with the remaining Gruyère and Cheddar and all of the Parmesan. Sprinkle evenly with the panko, thyme, and bacon, if using.

4 Bake until the tops are lightly browned and the sauce is bubbly, 12–16 minutes. Let stand for 5 minutes before serving.

Kosher salt and freshly ground pepper

½ lb dried short pasta, such as fusilli

2 tablespoons unsalted butter

2 tablespoons all-purpose flour

1 cup whole milk

½ cup half-and-half

Pinch of ground nutmeg

1 cup shredded Gruyère cheese

1 cup shredded white Cheddar cheese

2 tablespoons grated Parmesan cheese

2 tablespoons panko bread crumbs

2 teaspoons chopped fresh thyme

2 tablespoons cooked and crumbled bacon (optional)

Basic Pizza Dough

This is an excellent all-purpose dough that can be used for any pizza toppings you like. No need to call for delivery any more! You'll need to allow time for the dough to rise—that's when the yeast works its magic.

1 In the bowl of a stand mixer fitted with the dough hook, stir together the yeast, sugar, and warm water. Let stand until foamy, about 5 minutes.

2 Add the flour and salt and start the mixer on low speed. Slowly drizzle in the oil and knead the dough for 5 minutes. The dough should come together into a large ball and pull away from the sides of the bowl; it should be moist but not sticky.

3 Stop the mixer, remove the dough hook, and cover the bowl with plastic wrap. Let the dough rise at room temperature until doubled in size, about 1 hour.

4 Turn the dough out onto a lightly floured work surface. Dust a baking sheet with flour. Divide the dough into 4 equal pieces and, using your hands, roll each into a ball. Place on the prepared baking sheet and cover loosely with plastic wrap. Let stand at room temperature for 30 to 45 minutes, or if you will not be using the dough right away, refrigerate the dough balls on the baking sheet for up to overnight; then remove from the refrigerator and let stand at room temperature for 30 to 45 minutes before rolling out.

5 Place a ball of dough on a floured work surface. Roll out into a 10- to 12-inch round about ⅛ inch thick, dusting with flour as needed so it doesn't stick. Top and bake as directed in your pizza recipe.

2 teaspoons active dry yeast

1 teaspoon sugar

1 cup warm water (110°F–115°F)

2 cups bread flour, plus more for dusting

1½ teaspoons kosher salt

1 tablespoon olive oil

Mini Hawaiian Pizzas

This cult classic pizza is the perfect combo of salty-sweet. Deli ham gets a lift with sweet pineapple and a kick from diced red onion. You can also use leftover homecooked ham and fresh pineapple.

1 Place a rack in the lower half of the oven. Place an inverted baking sheet on the rack and preheat to 450°F.

2 Cut 2 sheets of parchment paper the size of a baking sheet and dust with flour. Working directly on the parchment, roll out the pizza dough into 4 rounds, each 10–12 inches in diameter (2 rounds on each parchment sheet). Divide the tomato sauce between the pizzas and spread evenly. Top each with the cheese and then the ham and pineapple, dividing evenly.

3 Have an adult help you remove the baking sheet from the oven; it will be very hot. Slide one piece of the parchment with 2 pizzas onto the inverted baking sheet and return it to the oven. Bake until the crust is dry and golden brown and the cheese is bubbly, 8–10 minutes. Carefully remove the pizzas from the oven and let cool for a few minutes, then top with half of the onion. Cut into wedges and serve. Return the baking sheet to the oven to preheat and repeat to bake the other 2 pizzas.

• •

Bread flour, for dusting

1 recipe Basic Pizza Dough (page 24)

½ cup No-Cook Tomato Sauce (page 66)

½ cup shredded mozzarella cheese

1 cup diced deli ham

½ cup diced canned pineapple

½ small red onion, diced

Mini Barbecue Chicken Pizzas

Topped with tender chicken mixed in tangy-sweet barbecue sauce, this pie is sure to become a favorite in your household. After handling raw chicken, be sure to wash your hands thoroughly.

1 Place a rack in the lower half of the oven. Place an inverted baking sheet on the rack and preheat to 450°F.

2 In a frying pan over high heat, warm the oil. Carefully add the chicken and cook, stirring occasionally, for about 2 minutes. Reduce the heat to medium, add ½ cup of the barbecue sauce, and simmer until the chicken is cooked through, about 8 minutes. Remove from the heat.

3 Cut 2 sheets of parchment paper the size of a baking sheet and dust with flour. Working directly on the parchment, roll out the pizza dough into 4 rounds, each 10–12 inches in diameter (2 rounds on each parchment sheet). Divide the tomato sauce and the remaining ½ cup barbecue sauce between the pizzas and spread evenly. Top each with the cheese and chicken, dividing evenly.

4 Have an adult help you remove the baking sheet from the oven; it will be very hot. Slide one piece of the parchment with 2 pizzas onto the inverted baking sheet and return it to the oven. Bake until the crust is dry and golden brown and the cheese is bubbly, 8–10 minutes. Carefully remove the pizzas from the oven and let cool for a few minutes, then top with half of the green onion and cilantro. Cut into wedges and serve. Return the baking sheet to the oven to preheat and repeat to bake the other 2 pizzas.

2 teaspoons olive oil

1 lb skinless, boneless chicken breasts, cut into cubes

1 cup barbecue sauce

Bread flour, for dusting

1 recipe Basic Pizza Dough (page 24)

½ cup No-Cook Tomato Sauce (page 66)

½ cup shredded mozzarella cheese

Sliced green onion and chopped fresh cilantro leaves, for garnish

With proper organization, the right equipment, and assistance from an adult, deep-frying is a cinch!

Buttermilk Fried Chicken

makes
4-6
SERVINGS

This fried chicken is delicious served warm or cold, making it great for a picnic or an after-school snack. Let the chicken soak in the buttermilk marinade overnight for an extra-tender bite under the crispy skin.

1 Place the chicken pieces on a baking sheet (thoroughly wash your hands each time after you handle raw chicken). In a large bowl, stir together 4 cups of the flour and 1 tablespoon each salt and black pepper. Toss the chicken to lightly coat with the flour mixture. In another large bowl, combine the buttermilk, the remaining 1 tablespoon salt, the remaining 1 tablespoon black pepper, and half the cayenne and the Tabasco, if using. Place the chicken in the buttermilk mixture, turn until coated, cover, and refrigerate for at least 30 minutes.

2 Remove the chicken from the refrigerator 15 minutes before frying. Preheat the oven to 350°F. Place a wire cooling rack on a baking sheet. Have an adult help you fill a wide, deep pot two-thirds full with oil and heat over high heat until it reaches 350°F on a deep-frying thermometer; adjust the heat to keep the oil at 340°–360°F.

3 In a large bowl, combine the remaining 4 cups flour, cayenne, if using, and the baking powder. Toss the chicken pieces in the flour mixture to coat. Have an adult help you fry the chicken. Working in batches, use tongs to carefully place the chicken in the hot oil, stirring if the pieces stick to each other. Fry, turning once, until deep golden brown, 10–15 minutes. Carefully transfer the chicken to the prepared cooling rack. Check the internal temperature of the chicken with an instant-read thermometer; if less than 165°F, roast the chicken in the oven for 10–15 minutes. Serve with the broccoli.

8 skin-on, bone-in chicken pieces (wings, thighs, drumsticks, breasts)

8 cups all-purpose flour

2 tablespoons kosher salt

2 tablespoons freshly ground black pepper

4 cups buttermilk

½–1 teaspoon cayenne pepper (optional)

½–1 teaspoon Tabasco or other hot sauce (optional)

Canola oil, for frying

1½ teaspoons baking powder

Roasted Broccoli (page 30), for serving

Roasted Broccoli

This unusual way to prepare broccoli—roasted with garlic and diced lemons—achieves a surprisingly complex flavor from just a few simple ingredients. Try it with other veggies, like cauliflower or butternut squash.

1 Preheat the oven to 350°F. Remove and discard the seeds from the lemon half and chop it into ¼-inch pieces, peel and all.

2 In a large frying pan over medium heat, warm 1 tablespoon of the oil. Add the garlic and cook, stirring constantly, until lightly golden, about 1 minute. Add the broccoli, lemon, 1 teaspoon salt, and a few grindings of black pepper. Cook just until the broccoli turns darker green in color, about 1 minute.

3 Scrape the contents of the pan onto a baking sheet, add the remaining 1 tablespoon oil, and toss to coat. Roast until the broccoli is tender-crisp, 10–12 minutes. Transfer to a platter and sprinkle with the cheese. Serve warm or at room temperature.

½ lemon

2 tablespoons olive oil

2 cloves garlic, minced

2 lb broccoli, trimmed and cut into florets

Kosher salt and freshly ground pepper

¼ cup grated Parmesan cheese, for garnish

Caesar Salad

This spin on Caesar dressing is creamy and rich without using raw egg or anchovies, so it will be popular with everyone! Serve as a tasty side salad or top with grilled chicken for a fresh and easy entrée.

1 Preheat the oven to 350°F. Line a baking sheet with parchment paper.

2 To make the croutons, trim the crusts off the bread and cut or tear the bread into 1-inch pieces. In a large bowl, toss the bread with the oil and salt. Spread in a single layer on the prepared baking sheet. Bake until golden brown, about 20 minutes. Let the croutons cool.

3 To make the dressing, in a food processor or blender, combine the garlic and ½ teaspoon salt and pulse a few times to chop the garlic. Add the lemon juice, mustard, sugar, and ½ teaspoon pepper and process to combine, stopping to scrape down the sides of the bowl. With the motor running, add the oil in a slow, steady stream and process until the dressing is creamy. Stir in the cheese. Season to taste with salt.

4 In a large bowl, toss together the lettuce, dressing, and croutons. Adjust the seasoning with salt and pepper. Garnish with cheese. Serve right away.

For the croutons

½ loaf coarse country bread

3 tablespoons extra-virgin olive oil

¼ teaspoon kosher salt

For the dressing

1 clove garlic

Kosher salt and freshly ground pepper

Juice of 1 lemon

1 teaspoon Dijon mustard

1 teaspoon sugar

¼ cup extra-virgin olive oil

1 tablespoon grated Parmesan cheese, plus more for garnish

4 cups chopped romaine or other sturdy lettuce

Fish Tacos

Panfrying instead of deep-frying the fish makes these tacos simple.
Any white fish, such as halibut, cod, or sea bass, will work in this recipe.
Leftover pico de gallo is great with homemade tortilla chips (page 48).

1 In a small bowl, stir together the paprika, cumin, garlic
powder, onion powder, oregano, thyme, 1 teaspoon
salt, ½ teaspoon black pepper, and the cayenne, if using.
Place the fish in a large bowl, sprinkle with the spice
mixture, and toss to coat. Let stand at room temperature
for 5–10 minutes.

2 In a large nonstick sauté pan over medium-high
heat, warm the oil. Add the fish and cook, stirring
occasionally, until just cooked through, about 4 minutes.

3 To assemble the tacos, fill the center of the tortillas
with the fish, then top with cabbage, avocado,
pico de gallo, and sour cream.

1 tablespoon sweet paprika

1½ teaspoons ground cumin

1 teaspoon garlic powder

1 teaspoon onion powder

1 teaspoon dried oregano

1 teaspoon dried thyme

Kosher salt and freshly
ground black pepper

¼ teaspoon cayenne pepper
(optional)

1 lb firm white fish,
cut into 1½-inch cubes

2 tablespoons olive oil

8 corn tortillas, each
6 inches in diameter,
warmed

Shredded cabbage, sliced
avocado, and sour cream,
for serving

1 recipe Pico de Gallo
(page 66), for serving

Sweet-&-Sour Shrimp with Mango-Cabbage Slaw

The sweet-and-sour sauce pairs perfectly with the sautéed shrimp and the crunchy fresh slaw. Increase the amount of chili sauce if you want to feel the heat. Serve this dish with a side of steamed rice.

1 To make the slaw, peel and pit the mango, slice it thinly, then cut it into matchsticks. In a large bowl, combine the mango, cabbage, and cilantro. Pour the dressing over the cabbage mixture and toss together. Let the slaw stand at room temperature for 15 minutes. Sprinkle with sesame seeds just before serving.

2 To make the sauce, in a small bowl, whisk together the broth, vinegar, ketchup, soy sauce, brown sugar, cornstarch, and chili sauce. Set the sauce aside. Peel and mince the ginger.

3 In a large nonstick sauté pan over medium heat, combine the canola oil, ginger, and garlic. Cook until the garlic is fragrant, about 30 seconds. Add the sauce, raise the heat to medium-high, and cook until the sauce is reduced by half, 2–3 minutes, stirring occasionally. Add the shrimp, stir, and cook until they are firm and slightly pink, about 3 minutes. Serve the shrimp right away with the slaw.

For the slaw

1 mango

½ head green or red cabbage, shredded

2 tablespoons chopped fresh cilantro

1 recipe Tangy Dressing (page 66)

Black sesame seeds, for garnish

For the sauce & shrimp

½ cup chicken broth

¼ cup rice vinegar

2 tablespoons *each* ketchup and soy sauce

2 tablespoons firmly packed light brown sugar

2 teaspoons cornstarch

¼ teaspoon chili sauce

2 teaspoons fresh ginger

1 tablespoon canola oil

1 clove garlic, minced

1 lb peeled and deveined shrimp

Slow-Cooker Chile Verde

If you don't have a slow cooker, a Dutch oven will work: Sear the pork and cook the onion mixture in the pot. Then add the rest of the ingredients, transfer the pot to a preheated 350°F oven, and cook for 2–3 hours.

1 Season the pork with salt and pepper. In the stove top-safe insert of a slow cooker or in a large frying pan over medium-high heat, warm the oil. Working in batches, sear the pork on 2 sides until well browned, 6-8 minutes per batch. Transfer to a bowl.

2 In the same slow-cooker insert or frying pan over medium-high heat, cook the onion, stirring occasionally, until translucent, about 6 minutes. Add the garlic and oregano and cook, stirring occasionally, for 30 seconds.

3 If you used a slow-cooker insert, return the pork to the insert and top with the chiles and their liquid, tearing the chiles into coarse strips with your fingers. (Thoroughly wash your hands after.) Then add the broth. Transfer the insert to the slow-cooker base. If you used a frying pan, transfer the pork and the onion mixture to a regular slow cooker, then add the chiles and broth as directed above.

4 Cover the slow cooker and cook on high for 2½–3 hours or on low for 4-5 hours, according to the manufacturer's instructions. The pork is done when it is tender and shreds easily with a fork. Adjust the seasoning with salt and pepper. Serve the pork with sour cream, cilantro, and rice or tortillas.

2 lb boneless pork shoulder, cut into 1-inch cubes

Kosher salt and freshly ground pepper

2 tablespoons canola oil

1 yellow onion, diced

2 cloves garlic, minced

2 teaspoons dried oregano

2 cans (8 oz each) roasted green chiles with liquid

1½ cups chicken broth

Sour cream, chopped fresh cilantro, and steamed rice or corn tortillas, for serving

Mini Meatballs in Marinara Sauce

The marinara recipe on page 67 makes a generous amount of sauce, so you will have plenty for leftovers. To ensure your meatballs will be tender, don't overwork the ingredients; mix them gently until just combined.

1 To make the meatballs, in a small bowl, stir together the bread crumbs and milk. Let stand for 10 minutes. Line a baking sheet with parchment paper.

2 In a large bowl, combine the ground meat, eggs, cheese, basil, parsley, oregano, garlic, 1 teaspoon salt, and ½ teaspoon pepper. Add the bread crumb mixture, and, using clean hands, mix the ingredients gently but thoroughly. Scoop out 1-tablespoon portions of the meat mixture and roll into balls. Place on the prepared baking sheet.

3 In a large frying pan over medium-high heat, warm the oil. Working in batches, brown the meatballs on all sides, about 6 minutes per batch. Transfer to a plate.

4 Add the meatballs to the pot of marinara sauce and cook, turning them occasionally and basting with the sauce, until cooked through, about 30 minutes. Serve right away with the orecchiette.

For the meatballs

1½ cups fresh bread crumbs

½ cup whole milk

2 lb ground beef, or 1 lb ground beef and 1 lb ground pork

2 large eggs, lightly beaten

½ cup grated Parmesan cheese

3 tablespoons finely chopped fresh basil

2 tablespoons finely chopped fresh flat-leaf parsley

2 teaspoons finely chopped fresh oregano

3 cloves garlic, minced

Kosher salt and freshly ground pepper

2 tablespoons olive oil

1 recipe Marinara Sauce (page 67)

1 recipe cooked Homemade Orecchiette (page 38), for serving

Homemade Orecchiette

It's lots of fun to make your own pasta, just like cooks do in Italy. Orecchiette, which means "little ears" in Italian, is a chewier pasta than most because it includes semolina flour. Made from durum wheat, semolina has a coarser texture than all-purpose flour.

1 In the bowl of a stand mixer fitted with the dough hook, combine both flours and 1 teaspoon salt. Slowly pour in ½ cup plus 2 tablespoons water and beat on low speed until the dough comes together. Continue beating on low until the dough is smooth and elastic, 5–6 minutes. Remove the bowl from the mixer, cover with a kitchen towel, and let the dough rest for 10–15 minutes.

2 Dust a baking sheet with semolina flour. Roll the dough into ropes about 6 inches long and 1 inch thick. Cut the ropes of dough into pieces ½ inch wide. Using the end of your thumb, gently press each piece to create a circular coin shape. Place the orecchiette on the prepared baking sheet and cover with a kitchen towel until ready to cook.

3 Bring a large pot of salted water to a boil over high heat. Carefully add the orecchiette and cook until tender, 3–4 minutes. Drain, transfer to a large bowl, and serve.

1 cup all-purpose flour

1 cup semolina flour, plus more for dusting

Kosher salt

Grilled Skirt Steak with Chimichurri

makes 4 SERVINGS

Skirt steak is one of the easiest and tastiest cuts of beef to cook. Topped with chimichurri sauce, the Argentinean sauce made with fresh herbs and olive oil, it becomes a perfect meal.

1 In a food processor or blender, combine the parsley, mint, capers, garlic, and vinegar and pulse several times to blend. Scrape down the sides of the bowl and season with salt and black pepper. With the motor running, add the oil in a slow, steady stream and process until the sauce is creamy. Adjust the seasoning with salt and black pepper and add the red pepper flakes, if using. Pour the chimichurri sauce into a small serving bowl and set aside.

2 Preheat a stove top grill pan over medium-high heat until just smoking. Generously season the steak with salt and black pepper. Carefully place the steak on the pan and cook, turning once, for 3–4 minutes per side for medium-rare, or until done to your liking.

3 Transfer the steak to a carving board, cover loosely with aluminum foil, and let rest for 5 minutes. Slice the steak across the grain and arrange on a platter. Serve with the chimichurri sauce. Store any leftover chimichurri sauce in an airtight container in the refrigerator for up to 2 weeks.

1½ cups fresh flat-leaf parsley leaves

½ cup fresh mint leaves

2 tablespoons capers

2 cloves garlic

3 tablespoons white wine vinegar

Kosher salt and freshly ground black pepper

½ cup olive oil

1 teaspoon red pepper flakes (optional)

1 lb skirt steak

Sweet Potato Fries with Herbs & Cheese

makes 4 SERVINGS

Sweeter than regular potatoes, sweet potatoes are delicious when oven-fried and tossed with fresh herbs and feta cheese. Feel free to get creative and experiment with different types of herbs and cheese.

1 Preheat the oven to 425°F. Rinse and dry the sweet potatoes. Cut the unpeeled potatoes lengthwise into batons about ¼ inch wide and 3 inches long.

2 In a large bowl, toss the sweet potatoes with the oil and a large pinch of salt. Spread the potatoes in a single layer on a baking sheet. Roast until tender and golden brown, 20–25 minutes.

3 Carefully transfer the sweet potato fries to a large bowl. Add the garlic, cheese, herbs, and a large pinch of salt and toss to combine. Serve right away.

2 lb sweet potatoes

3 tablespoons olive oil

Coarse sea salt

1 clove garlic, minced

2 oz feta cheese, crumbled

2 tablespoons chopped fresh herbs, such as parsley or cilantro

Garlic & Herb Pull-Apart Bread

Baking the bread in a Dutch oven gives it structure as it bakes and helps it stay moist. Serve this bread in the pot and let everyone pull off their own perfect piece. It's delicious dipped into Marinara Sauce (page 67).

1 In a small bowl, stir together the warm water and sugar and sprinkle the yeast on top. Let stand until foamy, about 5 minutes, then stir to combine.

2 In the bowl of a stand mixer fitted with the dough hook, combine both flours, 2 teaspoons salt, and ½ teaspoon pepper. Add the yeast mixture and beat on very low speed until thoroughly combined. If the dough is dry, add warm water 1 tablespoon at a time until the dough comes together. When the dough forms a ball and pulls away from the sides of the bowl, add the rosemary, thyme, and garlic. Raise the speed to medium-low and knead until the dough is smooth and elastic, 8–10 minutes. If the dough is sticky, add more flour 1 tablespoon at a time; if it is dry, add more water 1 tablespoon at a time.

3 Turn the dough out onto a floured work surface and knead by hand for 1–2 minutes. Form the dough into a ball, brush it with ½ tablespoon melted butter, and return it to the bowl. Cover with a kitchen towel and let the dough rise in a warm spot until doubled in size, 1–1½ hours.

1 cup warm water, 110–115°F

1 teaspoon sugar

2¼ teaspoons active dry yeast

1¾ cups bread flour

1 cup all-purpose flour, plus more as needed

Kosher salt and freshly ground pepper

1 tablespoon chopped fresh rosemary, plus more for sprinkling

1 teaspoon chopped fresh thyme, plus more for sprinkling

3 cloves garlic, minced

6 tablespoons unsalted butter, melted

4 Brush a 2- to 3-quart Dutch oven or ovenproof pot with ½ tablespoon melted butter. Punch down the dough, turn it out onto the floured work surface, and knead a few times. Divide the dough into eight 2-oz pieces and roll into balls. Dip the balls into 1 tablespoon melted butter and cover the bottom of the pot with the balls, then place any remaining on top. Drizzle the balls with 2 tablespoons of the melted butter and sprinkle with rosemary and thyme. Cover loosely with plastic wrap and let the dough rise in a warm spot until doubled in size, 30–40 minutes.

5 Meanwhile, place a rack in the lower third of the oven and preheat to 425°F.

6 Have an adult help you transfer the pot to the oven. Bake the bread for 10 minutes. Reduce the oven temperature to 375°F and continue baking until the bread is brown and crusty, 20–25 minutes longer. Carefully transfer the pot to a wire rack and brush the top of the bread with the remaining 2 tablespoons melted butter. Let cool for a few minutes before serving.

Soft Pretzels with Honey-Mustard Dipping Sauce

These freshly baked soft pretzels will change the way you think about this classic snack from now on. Soft as a pillow and oh-so-buttery, we recommend enjoying them warm from the oven. Make the dipping sauce while they're baking so you don't have to wait.

1 To make the pretzels, in a small bowl, stir together the warm water, honey, and yeast. Let stand until foamy, about 5 minutes.

2 In the bowl of a stand mixer fitted with the dough hook, combine both flours and 1 teaspoon kosher salt. Add the yeast mixture and beat on low speed until the dough is soft and smooth, about 5 minutes. If the dough is dry, add warm water 1 tablespoon at a time until the dough comes together.

3 Transfer the dough to another bowl, cover with plastic wrap, and let stand at room temperature until doubled in size, 30–45 minutes.

4 Meanwhile, in a saucepan over high heat, bring 3 cups water to a boil. Remove from the heat and carefully add the baking soda, stirring until dissolved. Pour into a shallow 9-inch square pan and let cool to room temperature.

For the pretzels

¾ cup warm water (110–115°F), plus more as needed

2 teaspoons honey

2¼ teaspoons active dry yeast

1 cup all-purpose flour

1½ cups bread flour

Kosher salt

⅓ cup baking soda

1–2 tablespoons olive oil, for greasing

5 Preheat the oven to 475°F. Turn the dough out onto a lightly greased work surface and divide the dough into 9 equal pieces for smaller pretzels or 4 equal pieces for larger pretzels. Roll the dough pieces into thin ropes and form each into a pretzel shape (see page 44). Let rest for 5 minutes, then place in the baking soda water for 2 minutes, spooning the water over the top of the pretzels if they are not completely submerged.

6 Lightly grease a baking sheet. Transfer the pretzels to the prepared baking sheet and let rest for 10 minutes, then bake until golden brown, 8–9 minutes.

7 Meanwhile, make the honey-mustard dipping sauce: In a small bowl, stir together the mayonnaise, both mustards, honey, and a pinch of kosher salt. Set aside.

8 Carefully remove the pretzels from the oven and brush the tops with the melted butter; be sure to use all of it. Sprinkle with sea salt and serve warm with the honey-mustard dipping sauce.

For the honey-mustard dipping sauce

¼ cup mayonnaise

2 tablespoons Dijon mustard

1 teaspoon whole-grain mustard

2 tablespoons honey

Kosher salt

3 tablespoons unsalted butter, melted

Coarse sea salt

Homemade Tortilla Chips with Guacamole

Try adding charred corn, diced tomato, and minced jalapeño chile to the guacamole for a Southwestern twist, or toss in some diced mango and jicama for a sweet and refreshing dip.

1 Preheat the oven to 375°F. Line a baking sheet with parchment paper. Stack the tortillas and cut into 6 triangle-shaped wedges.

2 If baking the chips, in a large bowl, toss the tortilla wedges with the olive oil. Place in a single layer on the prepared baking sheet and sprinkle with salt. Bake until golden brown, 10–15 minutes. Let the chips cool before serving with the guacamole.

3 If frying the chips, place a wire cooling rack on a baking sheet or line a large plate with paper towels. Have an adult help you fill a wide frying pan with ¼–½ inch of vegetable oil and heat over medium-high heat until it reaches 350°F. To test, using tongs, place a small piece of tortilla in the oil; if it sizzles, the oil is ready. Working in batches, use tongs to carefully place the tortilla wedges in the hot oil and fry until the edges begin to turn golden brown, about 2 minutes. Using the tongs, flip the tortillas and fry on the other side until golden brown, about 2 minutes longer. If they begin to brown too fast, reduce the heat to low. Using the tongs, carefully transfer the chips to the prepared cooling rack or paper towels. Sprinkle with salt while warm. Let the chips cool before serving with the guacamole.

8 corn or flour tortillas

2 tablespoons olive oil for baking, or 1 cup vegetable oil for frying

Kosher salt

1 recipe Guacamole (page 67)

To test if an avocado is ripe, remove the stem. If it falls off easily and you find green underneath, it's ripe!

Baked Chocolate Doughnuts with Chocolate Glaze

These scrumptious doughnuts get a double dose of chocolate—in the batter and in the glaze. Feel free to swap out the chocolate glaze with a vanilla one, and be sure to top the doughnuts with your favorite sprinkles. You will need a doughnut pan for this recipe.

1 To make the doughnuts, preheat the oven to 375°F. Coat the wells of a 6-well doughnut pan with nonstick cooking spray.

2 In a bowl, whisk together the flour, cocoa powder, espresso powder, baking powder, baking soda, and ¼ teaspoon salt. In a measuring cup, stir together the buttermilk and whole milk. Set aside.

3 In the bowl of a stand mixer fitted with the paddle attachment, beat together the butter and sugar on medium speed until light and fluffy, about 2 minutes. Stop the mixer and scrape down the sides of the bowl. Add the egg and vanilla and beat on medium speed until combined, about 1 minute.

4 Reduce the speed to low and add the flour mixture in 3 additions, alternating with the buttermilk mixture and beginning and ending with the flour. Beat each addition until just blended.

For the doughnuts

Nonstick cooking spray

1 cup plus 2 tablespoons all-purpose flour

½ cup unsweetened cocoa powder, sifted

1 teaspoon instant espresso powder

¾ teaspoon baking powder

¼ teaspoon baking soda

Kosher salt

⅓ cup buttermilk

⅓ cup whole milk

6 tablespoons unsalted butter, at room temperature

½ cup sugar

1 large egg

2 teaspoons vanilla extract

5 Pour 2 tablespoons batter into each prepared well. Bake, carefully rotating the pan 180 degrees halfway through baking, until a toothpick inserted into the doughnuts comes out clean, about 10 minutes. Let cool in the pan on a wire rack for 5 minutes, then invert the pan onto the rack and lift off the pan. Let the doughnuts cool completely.

6 Meanwhile, wash and dry the pan and repeat to bake the remaining batter in 2 more batches.

7 To make the glaze, pour the cream into a small saucepan, place over medium heat, and bring to a simmer. Remove from the heat and stir in the chocolate until melted. Transfer to a heatproof bowl.

8 Line a baking sheet with parchment paper. Dip the cooled doughnuts, top side down, into the glaze. Place them, glazed side up, on the prepared baking sheet. Serve right away with the glaze still wet (with lots of napkins) or let stand until the glaze hardens, about 5 minutes, then serve.

For the chocolate glaze

¼ cup heavy cream

¼ lb semisweet chocolate, finely chopped

Fried Lemon & Vanilla Bean Doughnuts

This is the stuff that doughnut dreams are made of—both tart and sweet and totally delicious. Fresh lemon zest and flecks of vanilla bean take these to a whole new level of fried goodness.

1 To make the doughnuts, in a bowl, whisk together the flour, baking powder, and salt. Set aside.

2 In the bowl of a stand mixer fitted with the paddle attachment, beat together the butter and granulated sugar on medium speed until light and fluffy. Add the lemon zest and vanilla bean seeds and beat until combined. Add the eggs one at a time and beat until combined. Then beat in the sour cream.

3 Reduce the speed to low, then add the flour mixture in 2 additions, beating until combined and stopping the mixer after each addition to scrape down the sides of the bowl. Turn the dough out onto a work surface, shape into a disk, and wrap tightly with plastic wrap. Refrigerate for about 30 minutes.

4 Line a baking sheet with paper towels. Have an adult help you fill a wide, deep pot two-thirds full with oil and heat over medium-high heat until it reaches 350°–360°F on a deep-frying thermometer.

For the doughnuts

3½ cups all-purpose flour, plus more for dusting

2 teaspoons baking powder

1 teaspoon kosher salt

4 tablespoons unsalted butter, at room temperature

1 cup granulated sugar

Zest of 1 lemon

1 vanilla bean, split and seeds scraped

2 large eggs

⅔ cup sour cream

Vegetable oil for frying

5 Meanwhile, if making the glaze, sift the confectioners' sugar into a bowl. Add the lemon juice and then the milk 1 tablespoon at a time, stirring until the glaze is smooth and spreadable. Set aside.

6 On a lightly floured surface, roll out the dough ½ inch thick. Using 2 different-sized round cutters (1 inch and 3 inch), cut out doughnuts and holes and transfer to a baking sheet. If the cutters begin to stick, dip them in flour.

7 Have an adult help you fry the doughnuts. Working in batches, use a slotted spoon to carefully place the doughnuts and holes in the hot oil, taking care not to crowd the pot or the doughnuts will fry unevenly and the oil temperature will drop. Fry, turning once, until golden brown, 1–1½ minutes per side; the holes will take less time than the doughnuts. Using the slotted spoon, transfer them to the prepared baking sheet. Let the oil temperature return to 350°F before frying more doughnuts. While the doughnuts and holes are still warm, dip one side in the glaze, if using. Alternatively, roll them in confectioners' sugar.

For the lemon glaze (optional)

1¾ cups confectioners' sugar

1 tablespoon fresh lemon juice

1–2 tablespoons whole milk

Confectioners' sugar, for coating (if not using glaze)

Safety Tip:
If the oil becomes too hot (over 365°F), lower the heat or turn it off completely.

Chocolate Pretzel-Dipped Cookies

Who would have thought we could improve upon the chocolate chip cookie? In this extra-decadent version, the cookies are dipped in melted chocolate and then sprinkled with crushed pretzels and sea salt.

1 In a bowl, whisk together the flour, baking powder, baking soda, and salt. Set aside.

2 In the bowl of a stand mixer fitted with the paddle attachment, beat together the butter and both sugars on medium speed until light and fluffy. Add the eggs one at a time and beat until combined, stopping the mixer to scrape down the bowl after each addition. Then beat in the vanilla.

3 Reduce the speed to low and add the flour mixture in 3 additions, beating until just blended. Stir in the chocolate chips. Turn the dough out onto a work surface, shape into a disk, and wrap tightly with plastic wrap. Refrigerate for at least 1 hour and preferably overnight.

4 Preheat the oven to 375°F. Line 2 baking sheets with parchment paper. Scoop the dough by tablespoonfuls and roll into balls. Place the balls on the baking sheets, 2 inches apart, baking in batches. Flatten the cookies slightly with the palm of your hand. Bake until the edges are set and golden brown, 9–11 minutes. Let cool on the baking sheets for about 10 minutes, then transfer the cookies to wire racks and let cool completely.

5 Line the baking sheets with clean parchment paper. Dip one half of each cookie into the chocolate shell and place on the prepared baking sheets. Sprinkle the chocolate-coated half with the pretzels and sea salt flakes. Let cool for 1 hour before serving.

2¼ cups all-purpose flour

1 teaspoon baking powder

½ teaspoon baking soda

1 teaspsoon kosher salt

1 cup unsalted butter, at room temperature

1 cup firmly packed light brown sugar

½ cup granulated sugar

2 large eggs

1½ teaspoons vanilla extract

1¼ cups chocolate chips

½ recipe Chocolate Shell (page 65)

1 cup crushed pretzels

Sea salt flakes

Fudge Brownies
with Peanut Butter Swirl

When a classic fudge brownie isn't good enough, we've got you covered. Imagine ribbons of salty-sweet peanut butter swirled through deep dark fudge. All you need is a glass of cold milk!

1 Preheat the oven to 325°F. Lightly grease an 8-inch square glass or metal baking pan. Line with parchment paper, leaving a 2-inch overhang. Grease the parchment paper but not the overhang.

2 To make the peanut butter mixture, in the bowl of a stand mixer fitted with the paddle attachment, beat together the peanut butter, confectioners' sugar, and salt on high speed until smooth and creamy. Add the melted butter 1 tablespoon at a time and beat until fully incorporated. Set aside.

3 To make the brownie batter, in a heavy saucepan, combine the chocolate and butter. Place over medium heat and warm, stirring constantly to prevent scorching, until melted. Let cool slightly.

4 In a large bowl, whisk together the brown sugar, eggs, vanilla, and salt until well combined. Add the chocolate mixture and whisk until incorporated. Add the flour in 2 additions and stir until thoroughly blended.

For the peanut butter mixture

2 tablespoons unsalted butter, melted, plus more for greasing

¾ cup smooth peanut butter

⅓ cup confectioners' sugar

Pinch of kosher salt

5 Spread half of the brownie batter evenly in the prepared pan. Dollop the peanut butter mixture by the teaspoonful on top of the batter, spacing the mounds about 1 inch apart. Spread the remaining batter over the peanut butter mounds and dollop the remaining peanut butter mixture on top. Run a butter knife or an offset spatula crosswise and lengthwise through the pan to gently swirl together the peanut butter and batter. Sprinkle sea salt flakes, if using, on top.

6 Bake until the top is set and a toothpick inserted into the chocolate part of the brownie comes out clean, 20–25 minutes. Let cool completely in the pan on a wire rack. Using the overhanging parchment paper, lift the brownie onto a cutting board and cut into 16 squares.

For the brownie batter

6 oz semisweet chocolate, roughly chopped

½ cup unsalted butter

1 cup firmly packed light brown sugar

2 large eggs, lightly beaten

1½ teaspoons vanilla extract

1 teaspoon kosher salt

1 cup all-purpose flour

Sea salt flakes (optional)

No-Churn Vanilla Bean Ice Cream

No need for an ice cream maker with this delicious no-churn vanilla bean ice cream recipe. You'll want to make it for every occasion! Try making decadent sundaes with Dark Fudge Sauce (page 62), Caramel Sauce (page 63), and sprinkles.

1 Fill a saucepan with water to a depth of 2–3 inches and heat over low heat until it barely simmers. In a heatproof bowl, whisk together the egg, egg yolks, and ¾ cup of the sugar. Place the bowl over but not touching the simmering water and cook, whisking constantly to prevent the eggs from scrambling, until the mixture is thick and pale in color, about 5 minutes. Remove the bowl from the pan and let the egg mixture cool to room temperature.

2 In the bowl of a stand mixer fitted with the whisk attachment, whip the cream, the remaining ½ cup sugar, vanilla bean seeds, and vanilla extract on high speed until soft peaks form. Gently fold the whipped cream into the egg mixture until completely combined, then pour into a 9-by-5-inch loaf pan.

3 Cover the mixture with plastic wrap and freeze until the ice cream is solid, at least 4 hours and preferably overnight. Serve or store in an airtight container in the freezer for up to 2 weeks.

1 large egg plus
6 large egg yolks

1¼ cups sugar

4 cups heavy cream

1 vanilla bean, split and seeds scraped

1 teaspoon vanilla extract

Dark Fudge Sauce

This fudge sauce is so delicious that you won't want to save it just for ice cream. Spoon it over fresh fruit or cake, or add a little warm milk to make the best hot chocolate you've ever tasted!

1 Put the chocolate in a heatproof bowl. Set aside. In a saucepan, combine the cream, corn syrup, cocoa powder, and salt. Place over low heat and cook, whisking constantly, until the mixture is almost at a simmer and the ingredients are well blended, 2–3 minutes. Stir in the vanilla.

2 Pour the cream mixture over the chocolate and let stand for a few minutes, then whisk until completely smooth. Store the sauce in an airtight container in the refrigerator for up to 1 week.

½ lb semisweet chocolate, broken into pieces

⅔ cup heavy cream

¼ cup corn syrup

2 tablespoons unsweetened cocoa powder

Pinch of kosher salt

1 teaspoon vanilla extract

Caramel Sauce

Ideal for drizzling over ice cream, this luscious sauce is a real treat. If you'd like a salted caramel sauce, toss in some sea salt flakes at the end. The caramel gets very hot during cooking, so have an adult help you.

1 In a sauté pan, off the heat, combine the sugar and ¼ cup water and stir, being careful not to splash the mixture onto the sides of the pan. Place over medium-high heat and stir until the sugar begins to dissolve, about 30 seconds. Stop stirring and cook until the mixture turns a deep golden color. If it begins to brown unevenly, give the pan a quick swirl or stir the mixture. Be careful because the mixture will be very hot and sticky!

2 When the caramel turns a deep golden brown, remove the pan from the heat and carefully and slowly pour in the cream, whisking rapidly. There will be lots of steam and bubbling! Continue whisking rapidly until all of the cream is incorporated. Add the butter and stir until dissolved. Let cool. Add a pinch of sea salt flakes, if using. Store the sauce in an airtight container in the refrigerator for up to 2 weeks.

1 cup sugar

⅔ cup heavy cream

2 tablespoons unsalted butter

Sea salt flakes (optional)

For a perfect dip: Insert a toothpick halfway into each buckeye, and gently submerge into the chocolate shell.

Peanut Butter-Chocolate Buckeyes

These are so easy and delicious, you'll want to make a batch every day. Save any leftover chocolate shell to pour over ice cream for a crunchy treat—just store it in the refrigerator and re-heat gently before using!

1 To make the buckeyes, in the bowl of a stand mixer fitted with the paddle attachment, beat together the peanut butter, confectioners' sugar, butter, and vanilla on medium speed until smooth. Scoop the mixture into balls, about 1 tablespoon each. Refrigerate while you make the chocolate shell.

2 To make the chocolate shell, in a saucepan, combine the chocolate, shortening, and corn syrup. Place over low heat and heat, stirring occasionally, until melted and smooth. Let cool to room temperature.

3 Line a baking sheet with parchment paper. Using a toothpick, dip the peanut butter balls in the chocolate shell and place on the prepared baking sheet. Sprinkle with salt and freeze for at least 30 minutes. Store the buckeyes in a single row in an airtight container in the refrigeratore for up to 2 days.

For the buckeyes

1 cup smooth peanut butter

2 cups confectioners' sugar

1 tablespoon unsalted butter

1 teaspoon vanilla extract

For the chocolate shell

½ lb bittersweet chocolate, roughly chopped

1 cup vegetable shortening

½ cup light corn syrup

Sea salt flakes

No-Cook Tomato Sauce

MAKES 4 SERVINGS

In a food processor, combine the tomatoes, oil, garlic, vinegar, and red pepper flakes, if using, and purée until smooth. Season with salt and black pepper.

Use right away or store the sauce in an airtight container in the refrigerator for up to 1 week.

1 can (28 oz) whole peeled tomatoes, drained

¼ cup olive oil

2 cloves garlic

1½ teaspoons balsamic vinegar

Pinch of red pepper flakes (optional)

Kosher salt and freshly ground black pepper

Pico de Gallo

MAKES 4 SERVINGS

In a bowl, stir together the onion, tomatoes, jalapeño, cilantro, and lime juice. Season with salt. Use right away or store in in an airtight container in the refrigerator for up to 4 days.

1 small yellow onion, diced

4 Roma tomatoes, diced

1 tablespoon diced jalapeño chile

2 teaspoons chopped fresh cilantro

2 tablespoons fresh lime juice

Kosher salt

Tangy Dressing

MAKES 4 SERVINGS

In a small bowl, whisk together the lime juice, vinegar, honey, and sesame oil. Adjust the seasoning with salt. Use right away or store in an airtight container in the refrigerator for up to 4 days.

¼ cup fresh lime juice

2 tablespoons rice vinegar

2 teaspoons honey

2 teaspoons toasted sesame oil

Kosher salt

Marinara Sauce

In a Dutch oven or other pot over medium heat, warm the oil. Add the onion and cook, stirring occasionally, until softened and translucent, about 8 minutes. Add the garlic and cook, stirring occasionally, for 1 minute. Add the tomatoes and their juices and season with salt and pepper. Bring to a simmer and cook until the sauce thickens, about 20 minutes. Stir in the basil. Use right away or store in an airtight container in the refrigerator for up to 4 days.

3 tablespoons olive oil

1 yellow onion, chopped

3 cloves garlic, minced

1 can (28 oz) diced tomatoes with juices

Kosher salt and freshly ground pepper

2 tablespoons chopped fresh basil

Guacamole

Cut the avocados in half and remove the pit and peel. Cut the avocados into 2-inch pieces and place in a bowl. Using a whisk, break up the pieces until they are mashed but not completely smooth. In a small bowl, combine the lime juice, cilantro, onion, garlic, and 1 teaspoon salt. Using the back of a wooden spoon, grind the ingredients until they are slightly broken up but are still mostly intact; this step can also be done in a mortar with a pestle. Add the lime juice mixture to the avocados and stir to combine. Adjust the seasoning with salt and pepper. Serve right away.

2 avocados

Juice of 1 lime

½ cup fresh cilantro leaves, roughly chopped

½ red onion, diced

1 clove garlic, minced

Kosher salt and freshly ground pepper

Index

THE JUNIOR CHEF COOKBOOK

Conceived and produced by Weldon Owen, Inc.
In collaboration with Williams-Sonoma, Inc.
3250 Van Ness Avenue, San Francisco, CA 94109

A WELDON OWEN PRODUCTION
1045 Sansome Street, Suite 100
San Francisco, CA 94111
www.weldonowen.com

WELDON OWEN, INC.
President & Publisher Roger Shaw
SVP, Sales & Marketing Amy Kaneko
Finance Manager Philip Paulick

Copyright © 2015 Weldon Owen, Inc.
and Williams-Sonoma, Inc.
All rights reserved, including the right of
reproduction in whole or in part in any form.

Associate Publisher Amy Marr
Associate Editor Emma Rudolph

Creative Director Kelly Booth
Art Director Marisa Kwek

Printed in the United States by Worzalla

First printed in 2015
10 9 8 7 6 5 4 3 2 1

Production Director Chris Hemesath
Associate Production Director Michelle Duggan
Production Manager Michelle Woo

Library of Congress Cataloging-in-Publication
data is available.

Photographer Maren Caruso
Food Stylist Jen Straus
Prop Stylist Kerrie Sherrell Walsh

ISBN 13: 978-1-68188-024-2
ISBN 10: 1-68188-024-5

Weldon Owen is a division of **BONNIER**

ACKNOWLEDGMENTS

Weldon Owen wishes to thank the following people for their generous support in
producing this book: August Abercrombie, Kris Balloun, Lisa Berman, Sean Franzen,
Gloria Geller, Alexa Hyman, Kim Laidlaw, Elizabeth Parson, and Alix Vaziri.

Williams-Sonoma wishes to thank the following kids for their help testing
recipes in the Williams-Sonoma Junior Chef Kids Camp: Amelia, Davis, Eve,
Grace, Jackson, Julian, Luca, Palmer, Reed, Rida, Ryan, and Taara.